EUROPA ⚔ MILITARIA №

ABRAMS COMPANY

Hans Halberstadt

and

Erik Halberstadt

The Crowood Press

First published in 1999 by
The Crowood Press Ltd
Ramsbury, Marlborough, Wiltshire SN8 2HR

British Library Cataloguing-in-Publication Data
A catalogue record for this book is available
from the British Library

ISBN 1 86126 285 X

Edited by Martin Windrow
Designed by Frank Ainscough/Compendium
Printed and bound by Craft Print, Singapore

Dedication:
For Michael Green, world-famous author and very good friend

Acknowledgements:
Since this book is based on the help and hospitality of many units over many years, I can't properly thank everybody who assisted in its construction - battalions of cordial soldiers and Marines have hosted me during live-fire and manoeuvre training at Twentynine Palms, the National Training Center, Fort Carson, and Fort Hood.

One person we must mention, though, is Bryan Whalen, a tanker with Bravo Company, 1st Battalion, 101st Cavalry, New York US Army National Guard who also works for General Dynamics Land Systems on the Abrams. Bryan has special insights into the tank as a result, and has served as our consultant on many details and issues about the tank and its employment.

I am also grateful to the marvelous Marine Corps, particularly Col.Michael Hawkins' 1st Tank Battalion down at Twentynine Palms. 1st Tanks has graciously hosted me on several occasions, allowing me to sleep on select portions of the Mojave Desert reserved for visiting media weenies - where the rocks are soft and the scorpions are smaller than usual, and well mannered. Lt.Dave Blankenship, Capt.Tunstall, Capt.Bolz, and many others from 1st Tanks provided accurate and timely supporting fires.

We likewise salute SSgt.Tim McDonald and SSgt.Jeff Dacus, both good combat Marines and veterans of the Great Drive-By Shooting. The essence of any weapon is its performance during actual combat, the acid test, and both Tim and Jeff provided their insights and experiences from Desert Storm. Atom Griego's incredible story of the destruction of his M1A1 Abrams and his narrow escape from death adds another important perspective on the vehicle and its employment in real-world combat.

The photos in this book were taken by the author unless otherwise credited. Readers may care to note that most of them are available from:
Military Stock Photography
240 South 13th Street
San Jose, California 95112, USA
tel:(408) 293-8131

Contents

Desert Storm: Warning Order

'Warning order for 3d Platoon: We will conduct an attack to seize hill at grid Echo Sierra five zero nine three zero six at zero seven hundred hours tomorrow. No movement before zero seven hundred hours. Ammunition and fuel will arrive at twenty-one hundred hours tonight. Hot chow at zero four hundred hours tomorrow. Pre-combat inspection at zero four thirty hours tomorrow. I will issue the operation order at my tank at twenty one hundred hours tonight.'

The true warning order for Bravo Company, 4th Tank Battalion, US Marine Corps had actually arrived well before their first combat, in mid-December 1990. Bravo is a USMC Reserve outfit, and was then equipped with old M60 Patton tanks. But on 15 December Bravo was activated, and quickly prepared for deployment to the deserts of the Arabian Gulf, and the venerable Pattons were replaced with new M1A1 Abrams MBTs. Within a few more weeks Bravo's 'weekend warriors' - teachers, salesmen, policemen, farmers, administrators - were checked out on the factory-fresh M1A1s. They rehearsed their battle drills, fire commands, SOPs; they wrote fresh wills and last letters to next of kin. For the purposes of the coming campaign Bravo got 'married up' to the infantry of 1st Battalion, 8th Marines, 2nd Marine Division.

By late February 1991 the five officers and 57 enlisted men of Bravo Company, 4th Tanks formed a cog in the whole massive machinery of the Coalition army crouched in the Saudi Arabian desert along the edge of the minefields forming the border with occupied Kuwait and Iraq. On the night of the 23rd

M1A1 'Rockin' Reaper' of 3 Platoon, Bravo Company, 4th Tank Battalion, USMC, parked up in 'The Pet Cemetery' at the end of Desert Storm, 1991. The direction of the painted chevron – forwards, upwards, backwards or downwards - indicated the four companies in the battalion; the three dots inside the chevron identified the platoon. (Courtesy SSgt.Jeff Darcus)

Bravo's tanks were lined up behind the combat engineers at Green 5 and Green 6, the easternmost lanes to be cleared in the huge minefield. The first tank, an engineering M60 with a mine plough, went across at 0458 hours, 24 February 1991, in darkness and rain. The first minefield was breached at 0636.

One of the engineer M60s was disabled during the breaching operation. It was pulled out of the way and the assault resumed, with Bravo Company's 1st Platoon in the lead. Sergeant Robert Trainor's M1, 'Four Horsemen', was out in front. Another mine detonated under a track; although the crew were uninjured the Abrams was out of commission and the lane was plugged, slowing the advance. Another lane was cleared by 0834 hours, and the remainder of the company moved out of the minefield and deployed quickly to support their accompanying infantry. The first objective was taken.

Late afternoon of the 24th found Bravo facing Iraqi infantry and armor, dug in and resisting. The company opened fire on the trenchlines and bunkers with coaxial and heavy turret machine guns. The resistance collapsed, and the enemy surrendered in droves.

(**Right**) Jeff Darcus atop the Reaper just south of the border prior to the ground war. Each platoon of Bravo Co. had a turret emblem: 3d Platoon's was this palm tree and 'USMCR'. (Courtesy SSgt.Jeff Darcus)

(**Opposite top**) The M1's 105mm main gun firing at night.

(**Opposite below**) Dug-in Iraqi T-55 destroyed by Cpl.Killian, the gunner in the M1A1 commanded by Sgt.Gibbert of Bravo Co., 4th Tanks. The APFSDS 'sabot' round's slim heavy metal penetrator makes only a small hole; in this case the stored ammo in the racks did not explode, but the shower of incandescent spall from the penetration would probably have been fatal to the turret crew. (Courtesy SSgt.Jeff Darcus)

Battle of the Candy Canes

Bravo charged past the defeated position. Cresting a small rise, the company found enemy tanks and other armored vehicles in a position near red-and-white painted towers. The long tubes of the Abrams' guns swung onto the enemy targets; Warrant Officer Larry Fritt's tank,'Hot Bitch', opened fire at 1650 hours, and the fight was on. Sergeant Glen Carter's 'Stepchild' identified an enemy T-55 tank way off in the distance - 3750 meters, two full miles away. He alerted his gunner with the order 'Gunner, Sabot, Tank!'; 'Identified!' came the response. 'Sabot up!' called the loader. 'Fire!'.

'Stepchild's' 40-ton bulk lurched backwards, then settled. A red dot raced away across the murky desert; and a slender, heavy dart made of depleted uranium struck the T-55 with such force that it melted a hole right through the thick cast steel armor. A hypervelocity spray of incandescent metal shards engulfed the turret interior; and instantaneously the ammunition stored in the T-55's racks detonated, enveloping the Russian tank in a fireball. The long guns were already searching the desert for the next targets. Staff Sergeant Tim Mcdonald recalls:

'I was a section leader, and my position was on the far left of our company advance. My gunner noticed something in the thermal sight and called my attention to it. I'd been standing up in the hatch, but dropped down for a look. I recognized it as a BMP, called the contact over the radio, and engaged. I lased the target - 900 meters - and hit it with a HEAT round. It must have been full of ammunition because it caught fire immediately and continued to burn for a long time.'

A few minutes later the fight at the 'candy canes' was all over: and Bravo counted ten tanks, four BMPs, four jeeps, 12 trucks, and a very dangerous ZSU-23-4 mobile AA gun destroyed. Nearly 400 enemy troops quickly surrendered.

Reveille Battle

That night Bravo formed a 'coil', each tank facing outward for 360-degree protection, with the CO's and XO's tanks in the middle. The tankers settled in for the night, watching, waiting, and occasionally sleeping. Half the company guarded the coil, watching through thermal sights and walking around the position, while one man on each tank was allowed to sleep.

Just before 0600 on 25 February one of the roving guards, LCpl.Stan Harris, woke Sgt.Tim McDonald - there was track noise somewhere to the front, out in the smoke and mist and darkness. McDonald alerted the company by radio, then started searching with the thermal sight. Over on the other side of the coil Cpl.Brad Briscoe was on watch inside 'Torture Chamber' when his thermal sight showed something moving out in the distance, about 4000 meters to the front - little dots of white against the green background of the thermal image, too far away for a positive identification. Briscoe popped out of the hatch and ran over tell his TC and platoon leader, Capt.Alan Hart, who was chatting with Bravo's company commander, Capt.Ralph Parkison.

'Probably just our own amtracs running around in front of us again', said Hart; 'Don't worry about it.'

Briscoe worried about it anyway. He told Hart's gunner to power up his thermal sight on 'Crusader' and to start scanning. The rest of Bravo slept on.

The clatter and rumble in the distance became louder. Parkison and Hart stopped talking and listened - that wasn't amtracs! Both officers raced back to their tanks. At 0550 hours Capt.Hart identified the noise as Iraqi tanks, moving toward his position over a distant rise in the terrain, down a hardtop road. 'Tanks! Tanks! Direct front!' yelled Hart, out of the hatch. Then he got on the radio: 'Stand to and come on line!'

Gummy-eyed drivers started up their 1,500 horsepower gas turbines; gunners switched on their thermal sights and began the two-minute cool-down cycle before they could be used. Off in the distance a parade of armor moved into sight and closed the range on Bravo's position. As the thermal sights flickered into life one gunner and commander after another focused on an amazing sight - a whole regiment of enemy tanks and armored personnel carriers emerging from the pre-dawn gloom.

Turbine engines came to life. Corporal Lee Fowble told his TC, 'Sir, we've got to shoot! They're traversing!'. Bravo quickly uncoiled, then struck. Captain Hart got the first shot off, engaging the lead vehicle at 1100 meters. The T-72 erupted in a fireball.

Over on the right SSgt.Jeff Darcus' tank 'Rockin' Reaper' came on line, the third of the company's Abrams ready for battle. His sight extension revealed eight vehicles blazing already - and lots of targets. 'Rockin' Reaper' opened fire and started killing an enemy tank with every shot. Tim McDonald: 'I began acquiring targets at the far left of the enemy formation, but as soon as I began to engage, suddenly the target would blow up and I had to find something else. That happened over and over ... I killed four T-72s that night.'

(Above) M1A1 with 120mm gun firing from a hull-down position behind a sand ridge. (Photo Greg Stewart)

(Opposite top) Iraqi T-72 destroyed by SSgt.Darcus' gunner, Cpl.Brackett, during the 'Reveille Battle'.

(Opposite below) Another wrecked T-72 on the 'Reveille' battlefield; note the trail of melted aluminum from the hull ahead of the dismounted turret. (Both courtesy SSgt.Jeff Darcus)

Within 90 seconds the lead elements of the enemy force had been blown away. Seven minutes after the first round screamed off over the desert, 30 enemy tanks and armored vehicles were blown apart and afire, littering the road. It took a while longer to police up the stragglers and survivors; after an hour Bravo counted 30 destroyed enemy T-72s, four T-55s, and seven smashed armored personnel carriers. Little Bravo Company - the 'weekend warriors' from Washington State - had destroyed an entire regiment of the feared Iraqi Republican Guard: 34 enemy AFVs, at a cost of no KIA, no WIA, and no battle damage to any of its tanks.

Sergeant McDonald was startled to see that 'Right after the engagement, the enemy soldiers started walking off the battlefield. We were pumped up on adrenaline from the tank engagement, and now we've got enemy dismounts walking toward us. We trained the machine guns on them, but it quickly became obvious that they'd taken a hell of a beating. Some were missing arms, legs - a lot of them were in bad shape. They surrendered, and we had to treat their wounded - no other units were in the area who could do so.'

The Battle of the L

After patching up the enemy wounded as well as they could, Bravo's tankers refueled, resupplied depleted ammunition racks, then moved out with their mechanized infantry. Late on the afternoon of 25 February, while making a 'movement to contact', lead elements of their task force encountered enemy mechanized and armored units. In gathering darkness, in foggy conditions made worse by a pall of black smoke from the oilwells set ablaze by the Iraqis, Bravo was ordered forward to take the point.

Corporal Vernon Forenpohar, commanding 'Torture Chamber', found an enemy BMP in his thermals and destroyed it. Staff Sergeant Jeff Dacus in 'Rockin' Reaper' engaged and destroyed a T-62 tank. Their objective secured, Bravo halted again, this time at a road intersection; on the map this road looked like a letter L, and so this nameless point on the map was christened.

Sporadic mortar fire fell on the position during the night, but without a good observer to correct the rounds it was ineffective except to keep the tired Marines awake. Tim McDonald decided to do something about it. 'That night was the darkest I can ever remember. You couldn't see the hand in front of your face. But while we were in this coil, we started taking sporadic mortar fire. This fire wasn't very accurate and we weren't really concerned about it as a serious threat, but we all got back inside the tank and buttoned up.

'I had adjusted my .50cal to be very accurate at 1000 meters. I noticed through my night vision sight that there was somebody out there at about 800 meters. He'd jump up, run a little ways, then flop down again. Then we'd take a few mortar rounds. The guy would jump up again, run back the other way, flop down again - and a few more rounds would drop around our platoon coil. It was obvious that this guy was the spotter for the mortar team - not very smart, but a spotter just the same.

'I opened up on him with the .50cal. You can tell, even in the dark, when you're getting hits with the IR (infrared) viewer because you see the warm tissue flying through the air. We checked out the guy later on, in daylight, and he was a mess.'

Then, at 0230 hours on the 26th, the Iraqis attempted to push through the position with tanks and troops in BMPs. It took a while, but by first light another nine T-72s, 12 BMPs, three BTRs, and one MTLB had been disassembled, their component parts scattered, still burning, across the intersection.

Welcome to the Pet Cemetery

After four days of nearly non-stop combat, with very little sleep for anybody, Bravo was ready to take Kuwait City with the rest of the force. Attacking through cultivated fields, then through an area of slums right up to the edges of the city, Bravo continued hunting Iraqi armor - but hunting season was now over. Saudi and Kuwaiti forces liberated the city, and the Marines and their battered Abrams tanks finally took a rest in a position gruesomely littered with dead cows, horses and zebras; the Marines called it The Pet Cemetery. Then they turned in their ammunition and their tanks, and went home to Washington State to resume their lives as teachers, salesmen, policemen, farmers and administrators.

The Marine Reservists of Bravo Company had accounted

for 119 enemy vehicles in four days, and had destroyed a whole regiment of enemy armor at a cost of no casualties at all. Much of that tremendous success was the result of excellent training, leadership, and the Marine tradition. But much of it was due to the amazing Abrams tank, with its complex systems and advanced armor.

The tank remains, 80 years after its invention and first deployment by the British Army on the Western Front in 1916, a fundamental element in modern land warfare. The tank doesn't win wars alone; but it has been the dominant battlefield weapon in the European campaigns of World War II, Korea, the Arab-Israeli wars, and most recently during Desert Storm in 1991. The M1 Abrams is certainly the best tank in widespread use today, and the best tank ever issued in quantity to any army.

'Whispering Death'

During the Gulf War - referred to as the 'Great Drive-By Shooting' by many veterans - the Abrams literally blew the doors off the competition. The M1 defeated the very best Iraq had to offer, outranging the vaunted Russian T-72 by a thousand meters, and able to acquire and engage targets through the darkest night, through oil smoke, dust, and rain. Though heavily criticized during its formative years (usually by armchair experts unburdened by first hand knowledge), the Abrams proved to be a durable, reliable, extremely effective weapon.

The M1 Abrams is a radical design in many ways. It uses a gas turbine engine, not a diesel, which is extremely quiet. On the move the rumbling and squeaking of the tracks is just about all that can be heard, and that only at close range. This, along with the thermal viewing systems, allows the Abrams commander to sneak up, seeing but unseen, on an enemy who has no warning of the Abrams' approach. In Iraq the first intimation that many defenders had that they were under attack was when they were suddenly taken under fire. Iraqi tank commanders standing in their hatches would have heard the crack-and-boom of American 120mm kinetic energy rounds splitting the air at a mile a second, followed by the deafening blasts of their own stored ammunition ripping apart nearby T-72s and T-55s, as their massive cast steel

(Above) The crew pose with 'Rockin' Reaper' on the day the war ended - on the glacis, Freier and Brackett; in foreground, Edler and Darcus.

(Opposite top) The Pet Cemetery, early March 1991: kill rings added to the Reaper's 120mm tube when the opportunity allowed - two T-72s, two T-62s, and a ZSU-23-4.

(Opposite below) An Iraqi T-59 abandoned within the Pet Cemetery perimeter outside Kuwait City. (All courtesy SSgt.Jeff Darcus)

turrets were tossed into the air like skillets. Enemy sabot rounds, when they were fired at all, bounced off the Abrams or embedded themselves harmlessly in its sophisticated 'Chobham'- type composite armor. No wonder the Iraqis called the Abrams 'whispering death.'

One man who may feel some professional sympathy for them is Atom Griego, who survived one of the most dramatic incidents of the armor war when serving as an Abrams driver with Alpha Company, 3d Battalion, 66th Armored Regiment. On the early morning of 27 February 1991 Task Force 141 was advancing deep into Iraq when things went terribly wrong:

'Being a tank driver is a strange job. You are alone with your experiences on the battlefield. The rest of the crew is back in the turret, busy with their responsibilities. If not for the TC's occasional commands - "Driver, left" or "Driver, right" - I could have thought I was in this alone.

'We went into action on Day 2 of the ground war, the 26th. After covering a lot of ground, refueling several times, we finally approached an enemy unit about nightfall. The Task Force commander ordered the tanks into line formation, with all of us abreast, and we attacked. Almost immediately bullets started to fly. Red tracers from American units, green from the enemy, filled the night sky. Our 120mm gun spoke with authority, making short work of Iraqi tanks.

'We pressed on through the night. About 0300 the next morning, after two days with almost no sleep, I finally began to

T-55 abandoned by the fleeing Iraqi occupiers on the Basra
highway in Kuwait, February 1991. (US Army)

get tired. I took a caffeine tablet and a package of instant coffee
- swallowing the tablet and pouring the coffee behind my lip like
snuff. I kept telling myself, "just an hour and a half till daylight
- things will be better then."

'Fatigue was taking its toll on the whole unit. The line
formation deteriorated as drivers wandered out of place,
sometimes into the line of fire of other tanks. My TC called our
company commander on the net, trying to get him to regain
control of the attack. The captain probably never heard the call.
At just that moment, one of our own units fired a sabot round at
my tank.

'It detonated square in the engine compartment, I found out
later. The blast threw me forward; I heard the loader, James
Hughey, scream, and then things went black. When I awoke the
fighting compartment behind me was on fire and full of smoke
and Halon. I wondered what had happened to my crew. Then I
heard a banging on my hatch. I managed to open it, and they
pulled me out.

'We escaped toward an adjacent tank from our platoon just
as another round struck our vehicle. Then we came under
machine gun fire, but it didn't last long - I guess they figured we
weren't worth it. They switched back to the main gun and fired
two more rounds into our tank. The ammunition caught fire, the
blow-off panels were blasted loose, and flames 75 feet high lit up
the area. We had a HEAT round in the breech and it cooked off,
burning two holes in the barrel. Our tank was a total loss.'

Five tanks were hit by friendly fire that morning. One
crewman, the commander's gunner for Bravo Company, 3/66th
Armor, was the only fatality.

Tank Units

The basic building block of a US armor unit is the tank platoon. 'Full-up' American platoons are normally composed of four tanks in two sections: Section One comprises the platoon leader and his wingman, Section Two the platoon sergeant and his wingman. Sections can operate independently, but seldom for long; two tanks do not have enough eyes or guns to protect themselves against all the possible threats hiding in the grass with missiles, swooping out of the sky with rockets and missiles, or clanking around a corner with heavy cannon. In practice even the four-tank platoon is vulnerable if it gets far from its infantry and artillery.

A typical tank company at 100 per cent strength comprises three 'line' platoons and one headquarters platoon, with a total of 14 MBTs, plus a 5-ton truck and a couple of HMMWVs ('Hummers') - the massive modern replacement for the old jeep. The HQ Platoon has only two tanks, one for the commander - a captain or lieutenant - and the other for his executive officer, known universally as the XO. The company first sergeant and the NBC (nuclear, biological, chemical warfare) sergeant use Hummers, while the supply sergeant and armorer follow the parade in the truck. On the rare occasions when the company is full-up it will field five officers and 57 enlisted soldiers or Marines.

The tank battalion will normally field four tank companies, plus many specialists in support. The battalion commander will generally be a lieutenant-colonel, his XO a major, and an extensive staff are assigned to a 'Headquarters & HQ Company'.

Platoon leader's M1A1 of 1st Platoon, Alpha Company, 4th Tank Bn., USMC - note single black spot in chevron.

The battalion will also have a heavy maintenance platoon, a mortar platoon, a scout platoon, a signals platoon, a FIST team, and many other assets.

At tank brigade level the mix of assets will depend upon the circumstances; but the brigade essentially consists of three battalions of tanks plus attached support elements. These latter will include mobile artillery in the form of M109 self-propelled howitzers, AH-64 Apache attack helicopters, and large logistics units with dozens of huge 'Hemmit' trucks for hauling fuel, ammunition, field engineering material and MREs to keep the tanks and tankers alive and moving.

As long ago as 1965 the US Army modified the shape of some of its organizations to return, in a sense, to the ancient cavalry concept. Horsed cavalry with their attached horse artillery were traditionally the component of an army that could cover ground at speed and - for at least a limited period - could operate independently. Modern US Army cavalry units, like the fabled 3d Armored Cavalry Regiment ('Brave Rifles'), combine armored and aviation assets - Abrams tanks and AH-1 Cobra attack helicopters - for a powerful one-two punch.

These Cavalry units use different terminology from

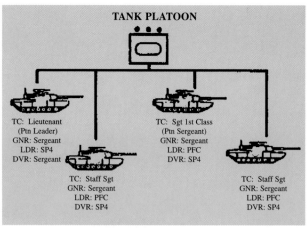

TANK PLATOON

TC: Lieutenant
(Ptn Leader)
GNR: Sergeant
LDR: SP4
DVR: Sergeant

TC: Sgt 1st Class
(Ptn Sergeant)
GNR: Sergeant
LDR: PFC
DVR: SP4

TC: Staff Sgt
GNR: Sergeant
LDR: PFC
DVR: SP4

TC: Staff Sgt
GNR: Sergeant
LDR: PFC
DVR: SP4

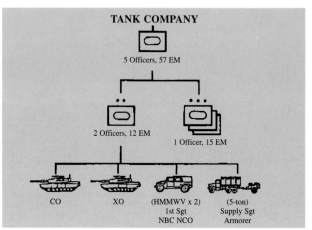

TANK COMPANY

5 Officers, 57 EM

2 Officers, 12 EM

1 Officer, 15 EM

CO

XO

(HMMWV x 2)
1st Sgt
NBC NCO

(5-ton)
Supply Sgt
Armorer

conventional Armor units. Cavalry units of company size are known as 'troops', whether armor or aviation. These troops are assembled into battalion-sized 'squadrons' combining armor and attack aviation. The squadrons combine with other units to build brigades – e.g. the 50th Infantry Brigade, a component of the 42nd Infantry Division, includes two mechanized infantry battalions, an armor battalion, another of artillery, and a cavalry squadron.

Tanks can be used 'pure', i.e. by themselves, or teamed with infantry following close behind in M2 Bradley armored carriers. This kind of tank-infantry teamwork is standard procedure for most real-world engagements. Only infantry can get into the trench-lines, among the rocky outcrops, and into all the other battlefield hiding places to dislodge enemy anti-tank teams, artillery spotters, scouts, and any other troublemakers. During World War II many tanks, on all sides, were taken out by heroic individual soldiers with short-range anti-tank weapons or even with magnetic mines and satchel charges. American tanks in the Pacific often had to 'scratch each other's backs' with .30cal machine gun fire, shooting off Japanese infantry who swarmed aboard with grenades and explosives. In the early phase of the Yom Kippur War of 1973 the Israeli Defense Forces had evidently forgotten this vital lesson, and their tank force on the Suez front was seriously thinned by Egyptian infantry tank-killer teams. No first class army will soon forget that bloody reminder.

The Armor Task Force

Even though Abrams platoons and companies can function alone, they very seldom do so in the real world. Instead, the tanks will fight as part of a large and complicated task force of complementary elements. These task forces are custom-designed for the problem at hand, invented for the moment by the brigade commander and his staff, and subject to change at a moment's notice. The commander mixes and matches all his resources as he thinks necessary, 'cross-attaching' units and sub-units so that in theory each group has the assets needed to overcome the particular threat it confronts.

Out at 'point' will be the scouts, in Bradleys on the ground and OH-58D helicopters above, prowling for targets and passing back information. The Abrams will be close behind, but with plenty of company. The Bradleys with their infantry will be a 'klick' or two back, ready to dash forward and clear bunkers or trenches. Attack helicopters will patrol the flanks like airborne horse artillery, engaging any threats in range. Well astern of the lead elements will be the mobile artillery, pausing occasionally to set up shop and launch their massive rounds over the top of the assault onto threats to its front and flanks. At 'drag', and struggling to keep up, will be the long logistics trains, the fuel and ammunition trucks, the big M88 tank recovery vehicles, the electronic warfare vans, and all the other specialist units.

(Opposite, top left) Marking for Alpha Co., 2nd Platoon. Note the turret rear bustle racks for stowage, which would be much fuller on active service.

(Opposite, top right) The basic 'wiring diagrams' - properly, the TO&E, Tables of Organization & Equipment - of a US Army Abrams tank platoon, and a company.

(Above) Platoon of M1s from 4th Infantry Division (Mechanized) manoeuvring in sections as they advance across the rolling terrain around Fort Carson, Colorado.

(Right) M1A1 section from the USMC 1st Tank Battalion on exercise in the Mojave Desert.

Brief History of a Revolution

Abrams tanks currently exist in three basic variants: the M1, M1A1, and M1A2. While all are very similar externally, each upgrade has brought major improvements. The original M1, with its 105mm gun, is now relegated to training, although many have been retrofitted to the M1A1 specification - these in fact constitute most of the Abrams tanks currently in use.

The M1 was developed to replace the M60 series tanks, a program that began in the late 1960s. At that time Soviet armor developments - first the T-64 and then the T-72 - raised serious questions about the future survivability of US MBTs on the battlefield. The T-72, with its innovative 125mm cannon, low profile, high-tech sights and laser rangefinder, caused particular unease among NATO planners.

The first proposed replacement was the MBT-70, a project whose cost and complexity caused a national scandal and attracted the ire of the US Congress. A rather more austere program was authorized in December 1971 under the designation XM1; the specification called, however, for a whole new level of both protection and mobility. Concerns over the potential cost led to several manufacturers being allowed to bid on the new design - a departure from standard procedure. The Chrysler Corporation prototype was selected for engineering development in November 1976; in 1979 approval was given for limited production, and in March 1982 Chrysler sold their tank division to General Dynamics.

The XM1 project was hampered, firstly, by hysterical media (and thus political) over-reaction to Israeli losses in 1973, some commentators even claiming that the day of the tank itself was past. This ill-informed press campaign dragged on until the beginning of the 1980s; meanwhile, there had also been some confused wrangling over a possible joint US/German MBT requirement. (Like most multi-national plans for the standardization of major weapons systems, this one foundered, as did a subsequent attempt to reach agreement over common component manufacture for the M1 and the Leopard II.)

The first production M1 was completed at the Lima plant in Ohio in February 1980, and the new MBT was type-classified in February 1981 as the M1 Abrams (named after Gen.Creighton Abrams, who had commanded the crack 37th Tank Battalion, 4th Armored Division in Europe in 1944-45). Deliveries of the first batch of production vehicles began in 1981. In 1982-83 the 2d Armored Division at Fort Hood, Texas, became the first formation to fully re-equip with the M1. By that time the brilliant success of the M1s of 64th Armored Regiment in the 1982 'Reforger' tactical exercises in Germany had already established its reputation as something revolutionary.

The M1 was designed to defeat the T-72 and its whole family. As delivered, the M1 offered greatly superior armor (the British- designed 'Chobham' composite protection), firepower (the versatile and hard-hitting M68A1 rifled 105mm gun), and mobility. One of the most interesting departures from conventional tank design was the use of the Textron Lycoming AGT-1500 gas turbine engine. Despite the howls of the skeptics, this proved to offer major improvements over conventional diesel powerplants including greater range, higher top speed (around 40mph), lower maintenance and quieter running.

(Opposite top) Tank platoon leader from the Georgia Army National Guard posing with his charger at the National Training Center, Fort Irwin, Califonia.

(Above) M1 of the 2d Battalion, 35th Armored Regiment, 4th Inf.Div.(Mech) at Fort Carson, Colorado, on exercise in the 'boonies.'

(Right) Rear view of an M1 moving up to the firing line for some range practice at Fort Carson.

The first revision to the M1, the M1 IP (Improved Production), had improved armor and added a bustle rack for non-critical stowage and an improved and redundant electrical buss, while retaining the 105mm cannon.

The M1A1, developed from 1986 with deliveries beginning in 1991, boasted the Rheinmetall-designed M256 120mm cannon, an improved fire control system with separate thermal sight for the commander, sophisticated hybrid NBC (nuclear, biological and chemical) protection, and improved suspension and armor. The addition of compartmentalized depleted uranium to the composite protection created the M1A1 HA (Heavy Armor) designation. This package represented a significant step forward. Both the US Army and Marine Corps used the M1A1 with great success in Operation Desert Storm. Units which shipped to Saudi Arabia from Germany had the M1A1 from the start, while those which came from the USA (except for the 3d Armored Cavalry) still had the M1 or M1 IP. (Most of these were replaced by reserve inventory from Germany before the ground war began.)

A further leap forward in capability was achieved with the M1A2 specification. By 1994 a major internal overhaul added highly integrated computer systems, greatly improved target acquisition and superior communications. Where the A1 is 90 per cent analog, the A2 series is 90 per cent digital. The A2 is equipped with 'hunter-killer' technology which allows the commander and gunner to simultaneously acquire and designate targets for the main gun. The TC can designate one target while the gunner is firing at another; as soon as the first is killed, the turret automatically swings into alignment with the second, and the gunner is ready to fire almost instantly.

At just a shade under 65 tons in the A2, with a 1,500 horsepower gas turbine and four-speed automatic transmission, the Abrams can achieve a top speed of 41 mph on level terrain (or even higher in some cases), and only slightly less in the bush. The 270-mile cruising range is more than adequate for most operations.

As of 1993, 4,796 M1A1s had been produced, including M1s which had been retro-fitted with the A1 upgrade. Some 377 M1A2s had been built or up-graded from earlier production vehicles, a program which continues. Egypt has bought 555 M1A1s, either finished or in kit form so that the Egyptians could learn the specifics of repair and maintenance. Kuwait purchased 465, and Saudi Arabia ordered 760.

(Opposite top) M1A1 of USMC 1st Tanks out in the Mojave Desert near Twentynine Palms.

(Opposite below) The M1A2; the most immediately obvious external difference from the M1A1 is the drum-shaped CITV (Commander's Independent Thermal Viewer) housing on the turret roof ahead of the loader's hatch. (General Dynamics Land Systems)

(Right) Fully stowed M1A2 of 194th Armored Brigade (Separate). Note the stack of nine smoke discharger tubes mounted centrally above the 120mm gun. (Photo Greg Stewart)

(Below) Compare this view of the M1A2 turret interior with M1 photos on pages 32 and 52. Note that the lens used for this shot, downwards and forwards from just behind the TC's position, creates a confusing false perspective: the width between the commander's instruments at left and right foreground appears the same as that of the whole fighting compartment. (General Dynamics Land Systems)

M1A2 ABRAMS TANK SYSTEM
TURRET INTERIOR

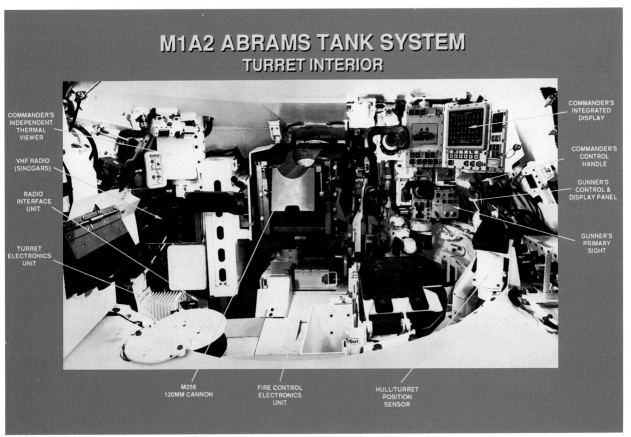

COMMANDER'S INDEPENDENT THERMAL VIEWER

VHF RADIO (SINCGARS)

RADIO INTERFACE UNIT

TURRET ELECTRONICS UNIT

COMMANDER'S INTEGRATED DISPLAY

COMMANDER'S CONTROL HANDLE

GUNNER'S CONTROL & DISPLAY PANEL

GUNNER'S PRIMARY SIGHT

M256 120MM CANNON

FIRE CONTROL ELECTRONICS UNIT

HULL/TURRET POSITION SENSOR

M1A1s of the USMC 1st Tanks on battle exercises in the Mojave. Marine Abrams have as standard a deep water fording kit, interface for PLRS (position locating reporting system), a mounting kit for a missile countermeasures device, and an external auxiliary power unit.

(Left & below) Headquarters tanks, their turrets - even the skate-mounted machine guns - swathed in desert camouflage.

(Opposite top) Abrams of Bravo Co. in a shallow firing scrape, the front of the hull concealed to some extent by a sand berm.

(Opposite below) The early morning sun strikes colorful effects from the sophisticated turret optics, but the TC's thick layers of clothing are a reminder of the freezing desert night.

23

(**Right & below**) M1A2s of Troop A, 3-8th Cavalry, 1st Cavalry Division out of Fort Hood, Texas, sporting desert warpaint. One Three Alpha carries temporary plates painted with its callsign in the turret side racks, and probably in the rear bustle rack too. (Photos Greg Stewart)

Walk-Around Inspection

M1A2 in temperate climate camouflage. (General Dynamics Land Systems)

Hull and armor

The hull of the Abrams is 30 feet long and 12 feet wide; from turret top to ground it measures a short 7 feet 9 inches. The M1 hull is carefully engineered to maximize efficiency and minimize battle damage. It is low, with sharply angled front surfaces to deflect incoming rounds as much as possible; these do the job well, even without the most advanced armor used in the front quadrant - the turret front and glacis plate.

The M1 was originally fitted with Chobham-style composite armor, a steel and ceramic sandwich originally developed in Britain in the 1960s. (Details are still highly classified; in the event of a penetration standard procedure is still to cover up the damaged area and immediately debrief all personnel.) To keep down the fighting weight composite armor is fitted only over the front 60-degree arc and other sensitive locations, the remainder being protected by conventional rolled plate.

Composite armor offers considerably greater penetration resistance and survivability than conventional rolled or cast armor. During Desert Storm the M1's armor met all expectations, resisting anti-tank guided weapons (ATGW), kinetic energy and chemical energy projectiles; of more than 1,900 Abrams in theatre, only four were disabled, and only one of these by enemy action. The usual effect of hits from Iraqi gunners was - according to one crewman - a scratch in the paint from a sabot round, or a small scorch from a HEAT shell. While some hits did penetrate the outer surface of the armor (for which it is specifically designed), leaving M1s with sabot rounds dramatically embedded in their hide, nothing the enemy threw at them did much damage even at close range.

The upgrade to the M1A1 in 1988 added depleted uranium (DU) to the composite, greatly improving the M1's ability to withstand most anti-tank weapons. DU is 2.5 times denser than steel; while raising the overall weight of the M1 to 65 tons, the new armor significantly increased crew protection and survivability.

One incident during the Gulf War testified eloquently to the Abrams' durability: US Army attempts to 'scuttle' a disabled tank at close range utterly failed. While US ammunition was capable of penetrating the armor and set off some munitions, the Halon fire suppression system took over to save the tank from further damage.

The driver's 'hole' is centrally placed in the front of the hull. With the turret locked in position, the driver's hatch swivels to the right and locks for entry or open-hatch driving. Army recruiting commercials to the contrary, you don't drive the Abrams with the hatch open in any kind of tactical setting - it is almost always 'buttoned up'. The driver reclines almost prone in an adjustable seat, under the turret drives and flanked by ammo and fuel storage and some of the electronics.

Engine

In the rear hull, separated by an armored bulkhead from the fighting compartment, are the fuel tanks and the power pack - the AGT-1500 gas turbine engine and Detroit Diesel X-11-3B transmission. An amazing 70 per cent of the engine components can be removed without removing the engine; or the entire assembly including transmission (called the FUPP, Full Up Power Pack) can be removed in about an hour. Removing a handful of bolts and unsnapping the electrical connectors allows the FUPP to be slid out, and the replacement unit slides right in. This is a major improvement over the diesel powerplants of earlier tanks. Although the turbine itself is more complicated to work on, keeping the parts count to a minimum and ease of R & R at unit level add up to much less 'down time' than with the M1's predecessors.

The Lycoming Textron AGT-1500 gas turbine is a major departure from old-school diesel propulsion. Developing 1,500 horsepower at 30,000rpm, it is run at peak efficiency, and road speed duties are delegated to the transmission. The AGT-1500 is a multi-fuel turbine engine; it can run on gas, diesel, or even aviation fuel. This means there are no pistons, rods, or complex gear trains. It is lighter by almost a ton than a conventional engine (and this weight reduction allows more armor to be carried). It is more reliable, emits less exhaust, faster, and much quieter than a diesel; and it will start even at -25 degrees Fahrenheit (-32 C), which brings it into line with the Soviet equivalent. All this adds up to longer MBTF (Mean Time Between Failures).

The turbine runs at constant RPM when above idle and as a result is always at maximum efficiency. It likes lots of well-filtered air, though not in quite the amounts of a diesel. During the early testing phase M1s proved the need for extremely efficient air filters and seals, as turbines are more sensitive to dust incursion than piston engines. Since the filtration issue was corrected reliability has been excellent; MTBF has almost doubled to about 600 miles (tank total, not just the engine).

With the arrival of the M1A2 and its enhanced electronics came the need for an auxiliary power unit (APU). This allows the AGT 1500 turbine to be shut down while at a prolonged halt, conserving fuel while the APU provides power for radios and electronics. Prior to the addition of the APU a bank of six 12-volt batteries provided limited auxiliary power.

Transmission and drive train

A Detroit Diesel X-11-3B variable speed automatic transmission transfers power to the final drive sprocket, with four forward and two reverse speeds. In case of turbine failure the tranny is left engaged, which passively drives the pumps for power steering and brakes down to around 5 miles per hour. The transmission handles all road speed control duties on commands from the driver's T-bar control. Failure to stop between drive and pivot or reverse can rather easily throw a track or blow a gear, however, deadlining the tank until maintenance can get around to repairs.

Experiments with hydro-elastic systems on previous tank designs had not been very successful, so a longer travel, more robust torsion bar suspension was tested and adopted as the

(Above) M1A1 of USMC 1st Tanks presenting its massively armored front quadrant.

(Opposite) An M88 ARV swaps an Abrams' FUPP in the field - a task which can be completed in about one hour.

standard for the M1. In part, it is the improved suspension that allows higher road speeds over both smooth and rough surfaces and greater reliability in bad conditions.

Tracks and road wheels

The M1 sports major suspension improvements over the M60. Fitted with seven road wheels a side and rotary shock absorbers on the first, second and seventh wheels, travel has been increased from 182mm to 381mm, leaving 4.65 meters of track on the ground. Alloy wheels are somewhat tender (read: breakage-prone), and tracks get inspected at almost every stop for loose connectors; throwing a track as a result of a dropped screw can really ruin manoeuvers.

Turret

The turret houses the majority of the weapons system, and all of the crew except the driver, in the 'fighting compartment'; it therefore gets the lion's share of the DU armor. It is capable of rotating 42 degrees per second and tracking a target at 4.2 degrees per second; elevation tracking speed is 1.4dps, to a maximum 42 degrees. This means a full rotation in just over eight seconds, or accurately tracking a target moving at up to 40 miles per hour.

The TC sits high on the right side of the turret, and has independent, stabilized day and night vision and a full 360-degree field of view with his hatch closed. The gunner's position is also on the right side of the turret, forward of and below the commander. The loader sits below the commander to the left, separated from the gunner by the breech of the cannon, with ready access to the ammunition storage racks in the 'bustle' at

(Above) In the dawn chill the engine louvers are a popular place to warm up both tankers and Meals Ready to Eat (MREs).

(Opposite) Road wheels and tracks of Marine M1A1s at Twentynine Palms. The heavy steel 'bazooka plates' protecting the upper part of the suspension are hinged so that they can be lifted for access.

the rear of the turret. The tank's radios are forward of his position; and mounted ahead of his hatch on the M1A2's roof is the CITV (Commander's Independent Thermal Viewer).

Most of the ammunition stowage for the main armament is in a rear turret compartment, equipped with powered blast doors held closed by a 'dead man's switch' operated by the loader's knee. Armor panels in the bustle roof are designed to blow off upwards and backwards in case of an explosion in the ammunition compartment, rather than allowing the explosion to vent forward into the fighting compartment. The M1 carries 55 rounds of 105mm, 44 in the bustle rack, of which 22 can be reached without leaving the loader's seat. Eight of the remaining rounds are carried in the hull behind the engine bulkhead, and three in the turret to the left of the cannon.

The changeover from 105mm to 120mm main armament brought a new case. The 105mm shells have a full-length aluminum case; the 120mm case is self-consuming except for a short base stub. Although the 120mm rounds are considerably larger, the weight for both is about the same at close to 50 pounds. The M1A1 amd M1A2 carry 40 rounds of 120mm, 34 in the turret bustle and six in the rear hull box; the compartment doors and blow-off panels were also modified.

(**Above**) This angle shows to advantage the huge overhang of the turret rear bustle.

(**Left**) Under the camouflage garnish the 120mm tube is 'lagged' with a thermal sleeve, to minimize the distortion which occurs during firing due to differential expansion of the steel. Gunners regularly check the alignment of their barrel and sights by means of the muzzle-mounted boresight (**opposite**).

Fire Control

The fire control system is one of the more innovative aspects of the M1. The combination of power turret and two-stage magnification for day or night use makes for rapid target acquisition and firing. While the gunner ordinarily has fully automatic systems available, if things do break down manual input for all major functions is possible.

The TC and gunner share two main sighting systems. The Gunner's Primary Sight - Line of Sight (GPS-LOS) has daylight optics with 10x and 3x fields of view. The gun has two-axis stabilization, keeping the the barrel pointed precisely at a target despite the movement of the tank. The gunner's field of view is a somewhat limited 120 degrees, so communication with the TC is important for target acquisition. With a 360-degree field of view and control overrides, the TC can either acquire and fire on a target, or delegate to the gunner.

For night use, and in dusty or smoky conditions, the A1 and M1A2 are equipped with a Thermal Imaging System (TIS). The TIS reads the temperature differences of objects in the field of view; this data is displayed in the gunner's eyepiece along with distance-to-target info from the laser range finder. The TIS combined with the two-axis sight stabilization allow target acquisition under extreme conditions at much longer ranges than previously. Neither night, dust storms, or chemical smoke screens can prevent the gunner from acquiring his target.

Although the fire control systems are extremely expensive, representing about 10 per cent of the total cost of the tank, they proved a real 'war-winner' in the Gulf, and a program of further improvement is in the works. Each of the sight systems is protected from 'incoming' by its own set of blast doors.

'Buttoned up', the only illumination inside the fighting compartment is the glow of the various control panels and a fairly useless dome light. Control panel illumination can be adjusted, and the sights have contrast controls so that the graticules don't overpower the target image.

Armament

As mentioned above, the M1's main gun is the rifled 105mm M68 based on the British L7A1 tube and American T254E2 breech assembly. This cannon requires low maintenance, is highly accurate out to 2,500 meters, and can handle a variety of projectiles. The M1A1 and M1A2 mount the smooth-bore 120mm M256, effective out to around 3,000 meters.

The two main types of projectiles are CE (Chemical Energy) shaped charge rounds, and KE (Kinetic Energy) penetrators. The CE rounds are referred to as HEAT (High Explosive Anti-Tank); these deliver a tightly focussed explosive charge, penetrating the armor plate on the enemy vehicle. HEAT rounds travel somewhat slower than sabot, with a higher trajectory.

Kinetic energy rounds comprise a thin rod of tungsten or DU encased in a 'sabot' to fit the bore of the cannon; this breaks away after the projectile leaves the muzzle. Fired from an unrifled tube, the projectile does not spin, and so requires small fins to stabilize its flight (hence Armor Piercing Fin Stabilized Discarding Sabot - APFSDS). The penetrator is delivered at high velocity, about a mile per second, punching a small, very clean hole in the target armor; field reports say that it looks as if it was done with a welder's torch. The friction of the rod passing through armor melts the rod, turning it into a spray of superheated molten metal which continues to inflict severe damage inside the tank.

One M240 7.62mm machine gun is coaxially mounted on the right side of the main gun, and shares the Gunner's Primary Sight (GPS) and the Gunner's Auxiliary Sight (GAS). A second M240 is skate-mounted at the loader's hatch; 11,400 rounds of 7.62mm can be carried. The M240 features three controlled rates of fire: 650-950 rounds cyclic, 200rpm rapid fire, and a sustained rate of 100rpm (firing more than 200rpm may cause the gun to overheat.) Weighing in at 24lbs, the M240 has a maximum effective range of just over a mile.

One M2 .50cal (12.7mm) Browning heavy machine gun with a 3x magnification sight is fitted on a power-traversed, manually-elevated mount ahead of the commander's cupola. This classic World War II era design is belt-fed, recoil-operated and air-cooled; it is highly effective against thin-skinned vehicles, personnel and aircraft. It can be aimed and fired manually, or remotely from 'under armor'; in the M1A2 it is fitted with a solenoid trigger mechanism, replacing the more difficult mechanical trigger used on earlier models. As produced by Saco Defense, it weighs 84lbs plus mount, fires 550rpm, and has a maximum effective range of 2,000m (about a mile and a quarter); 1,000 rounds are carried.

A six-barrel M250 smoke discharger is mounted on either side of the turret of the M1 and M1A1; an additional cluster has been seen centrally mounted above the main gun of some A2s. The A1 and A2 also have an engine-operated smoke generator.

The M1A1 and A2 are protected against nuclear, biological and chemical threats; they are equipped with a 200 SCFM clean conditioned air system, an AN/VDR-1 Radiac radiological warning device, and a chemical agent detector. The crew are equipped with protective suits and facemasks and, in the A2, with air-conditioned vests for hot weather operations in NBC conditions which require zero-exposure clothing.

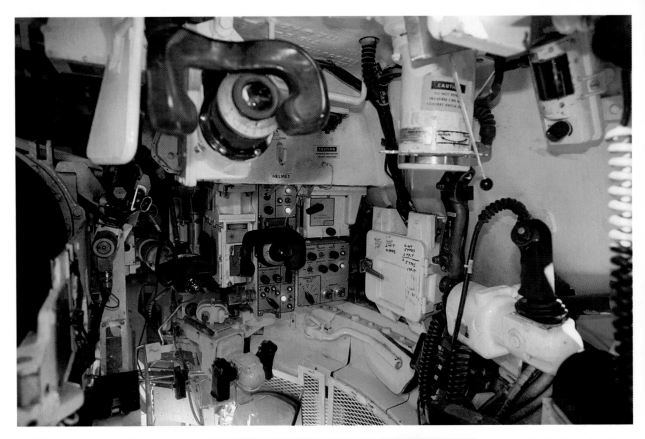

(**Above & left**) Gunner's station of the M1 Abrams, with and without occupant.

(**Opposite**) The 105mm main gun firing - a memorable experience when standing in the open at close quarters.

While the 105mm may be capable of reaching out to make kills at 3,000m, and the 120mm perhaps even out to an extraordinary 5,000m, in practice the sights limit the effective range. At 3,000m the target fills the sight, and the graticule can be so bright that it obscures the objective. Engagement usually takes place at ranges between 500m and 1,500m, and first-round kills are expected out to around 2,500 meters.

The Human Factor

An M1 Abrams series tank costs the US government several million dollars; but the effectiveness and the survival in battle of this 65-ton technical marvel depends on four Mk I human beings, whose design has not changed significantly in fifty thousand years. Married up to the systems in their M1, they can cost an enemy government three or four times the price of a modern tank, plus the total expended cost of training and paying 12 or 16 soldiers, in 60 to 90 seconds of furious activity.

The loader

An apprentice tanker fresh out of Armor School at Fort Knox, Kentucky, begins his practical education as the loader. His primary assignment is 'serving' the cannon during engagements. Both the tank commander (TC) and the loader will normally stand in their hatches when not actually engaged in combat, during 'movement to contact'; the loader, manning his M240 7.62mm machine gun, scans the ground and sky to the left side and rear for hostile aircraft, infantry anti-tank teams, and vehicles.

The driver

After a few months as a loader a soldier is likely to get a chance to serve as the driver. (The driver and loader will often trade places, particularly on long road marches, to keep both alert and to give the loader some experience at the helm.) The basic operation of the tank is simple and natural to anybody who has ever driven a car. The Abrams is one of the easiest tanks to drive ever built, but the simplicity of the basic controls does not mean that the driver's job is easy. He has to be able to read the commander's mind, to position the tank where it needs to be without being constantly instructed - and without getting stuck in an obstacle or breaking a track. He has to be constantly aware of the lie of the land in case he needs to get under cover fast. He is also tasked with helping the gunner and TC evaluate the accuracy and effect of fire from the main gun.

The gunner

Tucked deep into the bowels of the tank, with only a very narrow view of the world outside, the gunner is normally a sergeant E-5 or platoon sergeant E-6 with several years' experience in tanks and extensive formal and informal training in gunnery.

Although the Abrams fire control system automates many of the readings, calculations and adjustments required for accurate long-range fire, the gunner has to combine the skills of a computer technician with those of a traditional marksman. A good gunner is quite properly revered by the other members of his unit, and a very good one may be designated Master Gunner of the battalion.

The commander

The tank commander (TC) will typically be an experienced sergeant or a young lieutenant platoon leader. His primary responsibility is insuring that the tank and its crew play their role in the tactical plan. If he is the platoon leader he will spend most of his time searching for threats and targets, co-ordinating with adjacent units, navigating, sending spot reports, and trying to stay out of trouble. All three other tanks in the platoon will normally mimic everything the platoon leader does in accordance with the 'wingman' concept, adapted from 'finger four' fighter aircraft tactics.

It's difficult to really appreciate any complex weapon system without actually climbing aboard; so put on your boots, tanker's coveralls and Helmet, Combat Vehicle Crewman (CVC), and we'll check you out on the Abrams' four crew positions and duties.

(Right) A muffled crewman of USMC 1st Tanks, cuddling a 120mm round atop his M1A1 turret during freezing exercises near Yakima, Washington State. His gear recalls the old 'bib-and-suspenders' winter clothing issued to tankers in World War II. (Courtesy Lt.Chris Brown)

(Below) Creative application of camouflage cream by Chris Brown's crew from 1st Tanks: LCpls.Melville (loader), Grass (gunner) and Vaughn (driver). Each crewman has carefully defined duties, and the whole crew is trained in and practices individual and collective skills until they become nearly automatic. The driver is responsible for general vehicle and track maintenance; the gunner, for the care and maintenance of the weapons systems. He is also the assistant commander of the tank, and can take over if the TC is absent or becomes a casualty. (Courtesy Lt.Chris Brown)

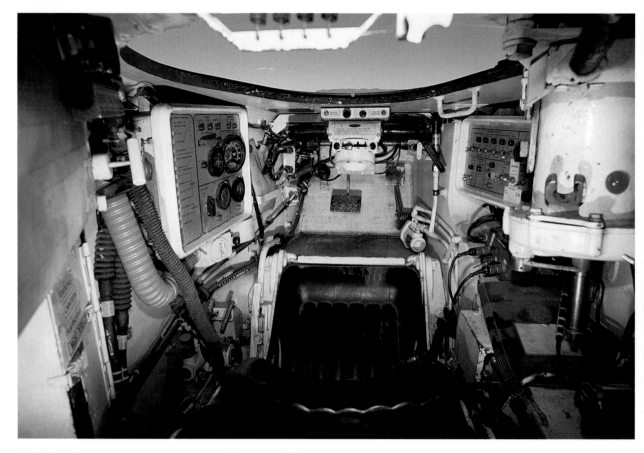

Welcome to the Crew

The driver

You will normally be the first man aboard. You climb up at the front left of the tank, using a stirrup and handhold on the track shield. Then clamber up on top of the turret, and drop through the loader's hatch onto his seat, and then to the turret floor. The only way to get into the driver's compartment is to squirm through feet first, past the left side of the gun. (The turret must have the gun traversed to the rear if you're to have access this way.) The seat back should be down and the headrest up, allowing you to slide in. You'll be almost flat on your back, in the dark, so you need to know where everything is by feel and experience. Adjust the seat and headrest for comfort, then plug in your CVC headset jack. The driver's normal pre-operation checklist is more detailed than you need to know right now, so we'll stick to the basics:

The Master Power switch is on a panel on the Driver's Master Panel to your right. All the top switches should be off, fire extinguisher Tank Selector to REAR, 2nd Shot switch cover closed, all gauges at zero or minimum indications. Pull out and lift the Master Power switch to ON and its light will illuminate. Press and hold Master Caution test button - all indicators should light up, then go out when the button is released. Check that the needle of the electrical system gauge is in the green.

Make sure the periscopes are adjusted so you can see the terrain to the front and sides clearly, with a minimum of head movement. Then adjust the steering/throttle control by pulling out the knob on the left side, positioning the control to suit yourself. Release the knob and it locks. You're almost ready to start; normally, you now call the TC on your ICS to verify that nobody is behind the tank. Make sure the transmission control, in the center of the steering/throttle control, is set to NEUTRAL. The TC should insure that turret power is OFF.

Now you simply press the engine start switch on the right side panel and hold it for about three seconds. You'll hear the sound of the turbine engine spinning up to speed, then a *whoosh* as it automatically lights off. After a minute or so the RPM should settle down at about 900 to 920, the electrical gauge should show output at around 28 volts, and you should see no warning lights. You're 'good to go'. The actual operation of the Abrams should come simply and naturally to anyone who has ever driven a car with automatic transmission, though the hand controls are more like those of a motorcycle.

Just as with a car, step on the brake (right where it belongs) and shift into the normal drive range, the 'D' on the control. Throttle control is by twist grips;

(Above & opposite top) Driver's compartment with hatch open; and 'buttoned up', showing the three periscopes - the middle one can be replaced by an image-intensifying night driving scope.

(Opposite bottom) Driver at the helm, with headrest down.

release the brake and gradually apply throttle. 'Driver, move out!' - and the TC will tell you where he wants to go. Visibility is quite restricted and you need to be vigilant for other vehicles, rocks, holes and other hazards. The brakes are good enough to stop the tank on a large dime, but the crew will not appreciate being slammed around. Driving cross-country in a tactical area requires skill and experience. Normally you'll be part of a formation, keeping station with a tank on your left or right front. At the same time you

(continued on page 38)

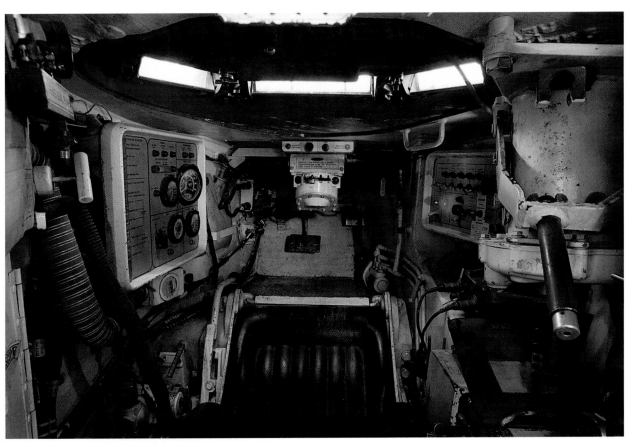

must be aware of the terrain ahead, and on the lookout for places along the route offering cover or concealment should you come under fire. The Abrams is quite capable of charging across the desert at 45mph - which makes it all too easy for you to smash roadwheels on a hidden rock, break a track in a sudden turn, or drive the tank into something deep and expensive.

There are both perks and drawbacks to the driver's job. He has the best seat in the house, and is always more comfortable than the rest of the crew. He has the personnel heater control, and can stay warm when everybody else is freezing. When it's time to sleep the rest of the crew have to set up their bags on the ground or on the back deck, exposed to the elements - none of them can get comfortable inside the turret. The driver is already lying down on the job, and can sleep reasonably well right where he is.

The downside for the driver is that he is isolated in his frontal compartment, for better or worse. In an emergency the turret must be turned to six-o'clock to allow him to climb back out the way he got in - the gun can easily block his access through the hatch.

The loader

All acolyte tankers learn their trade beginning at the loader's station in the left rear of the turret. You sit in the left rear corner of the fighting compartment, facing across the gun breech towards the TC. On his or the gunner's command, you extract a HEAT or sabot round from the ammunition stowage compartment and feed it to the gun (see pages 40-41).

(1)
There's a large flat switch at knee level; on the command, press it with your right knee and the ballistic panel will slide open, revealing the rounds in their bins – the bases are marked H or S, indicating the type of round.

(2)
The bins are spring-loaded, so push in with your right fist, then release - the base of the round will pop out a few inches.

(3)
Extract the round and pivot to your left, toward the gun breech; as you release pressure on the knee switch the ballistic door will close. Feed the nose of the round into the breech; then make a fist with your right hand, and push the round all the way home into the chamber. When it is fully seated the extractors will trip and the breechblock will slam shut; using your fist helps avoid getting your fingers mangled.

(4)
Now swing the ejection guard to the rear; check to ensure the yellow ARMED light illuminates; then call 'Up!' on the ICS (Internal Communication System) to let the rest of the crew know the gun is ready to fire.

(**Above**) A practice 105mm APFSDS or 'sabot' round disassembled, with the slim penetrator separated from the halves of the sabot which is discarded after the round leaves the muzzle.

(**Left**) Again, blue paint identifies a 105mm drill round - this one a flat-headed HEAT shell with a protruding detonator, to set off the shaped charge of high explosive a nano-second before the main projectile hits the target's armor. Combat rounds are painted black.

The loading sequence described on page 39: this is not a job that requires a lot of initiative - you do what you're told, immediately. It does take a lot of upper body strength, however, to pop a 55lb round out of its storage rack, flip it end for end, and ram it home in the breech in under five seconds. It also takes agility to perform this task on the move across country, when the tank is bucketing over rough ground and the big breech of the stabilized gun is rising and sinking with a mind of its own; bruises, cracked ribs or fractures can be the price of clumsiness.

Safe handling of the ammunition is also a primary concern. Main gun rounds are ignited by a 1.5 volt charge; and since the hull carries 12 volts, setting down or dropping a round on its base risk the propellant igniting. Accidents have happened, and loaders learn to treat the big shells with great respect.

(Left) 105mm sabot round in the breech of the M68A1 gun.

(Below) The breechblock closing. In this sequence of photos the loader's roof hatch is open for the sake of light; in action it would be locked, and he would have to perform his task in much greater gloom.

'I've seen people "vacuum load" 105 rounds, but I don't recommend it, and it is against our SOPs; but in a pinch, when you have to re-engage in a very short period of time, it is great to have a loader who can do that. The minimum standard is under five seconds, and I have done it in three and a half, but there are guys who do it faster. When the TC commands, "Gunner-Sabot- Tank!" the loader hits the switch, grabs the round, slams it into the breech, swings the arming lever, and calls "Up!", and does it all in under three seconds - he's just a blur! But if you sit there and do it enough times, you get the movements down and you become mechanical.'

The loader needs to be very strong, very quick, and very humble; he's at the bottom of the crew food chain, and gets tapped for every dirty detail. If ever somebody needs to go fetch something, it will be the loader who gets the call. It isn't really a desirable position.

On the other hand, unlike the gunner, he does get to enjoy the fresh air and scenery while standing in his hatch during 'movement to contact' (also the blazing desert sun and choking dust; turret-high flying mud; or freezing winter wind and rain). In a tactical situation constant vigilance is essential; the first warning the loader might get is the flash and dust cloud signature of an anti-tank missile launch headed in their direction, or the bug-eyed front view of an Mi-24 Hind attack helicopter popping up from behind a ridge.

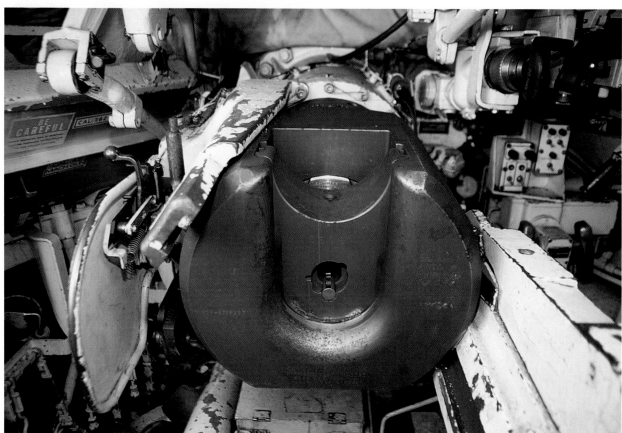

(**Above & right**) When it's time to replenish the ammunition bins the whole crew may help out. Despite the great advances made in recent years with all kinds of palletized stores and the specialist vehicles to load and unload them automatically, there is still no way to get tank shells off a truck and down through the hatches except by manhandling them one by one. Here Marines of 4th Tanks take on 120mm rounds - above, a HEAT practice round, and right, APFSDS. Note the different colors showing the junction between the self-consuming case and the short base stub which is ejected from the breech after firing. This photo also shows detail of the loader's hatch and periscope, and the mount for his M240.

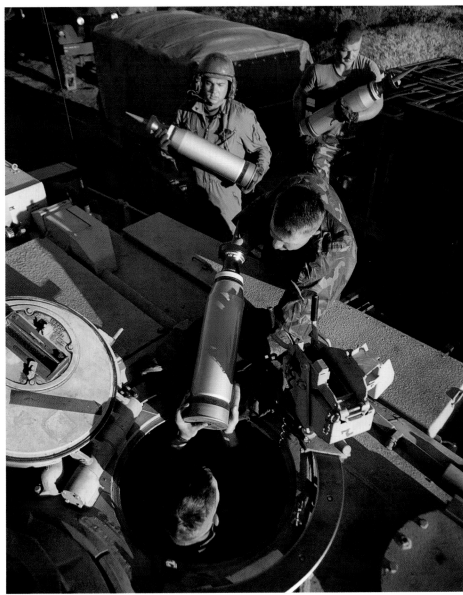

The gunner

(Above) Marine gunner in M1A1 of 1st Tank Bn. **(Right)** Close-up of sight eyepieces and some of the gunner's control panels in the M1. **(Opposite)** Detail of the chest brace and Cadillacs in use.

Over on the right side of the gun breech, in front of the TC, is the gunner's complex duty station. Worm your way in from either the loader's or TC's hatch, sit down, and adjust the seat. This is unique in the tank, and is designed to lock you into the sight systems and allow you to work despite the rock and roll when the M1 is crossing rough terrain. A chest brace locks into place in front of you, helping you avoid smashing your face on the sights and weapons controls. In motion you must learn to brace your feet to press your lower back against the seat, leaning forward against the chest piece,

with your helmet jammed against the pads around the primary sight and holding on to the main gun power control handles (built by Cadillac-Gage Corps., and known by all as the 'Cadillacs').

In front of you are two sights: the GPS, Gunner's Primary Sight, and the GAS, Gunner's Auxiliary Sight. Below them are the control panels for the thermal sight, fire control mode switch, gun select switch (cannon or coax), and ammunition select switch (HEAT, BH, HEP, SABOT). To your immediate right is the ballistic computer panel in which you enter such factors as ammunition temperature, tank tilt or 'cant' angle, barometric pressure, air temperature, and other factors.

The gunner's job is easily the most complicated and technical, and a full description of his systems and their operation could fill this entire book. Instead, let's just fire a few rounds downrange and see if we can hit something.

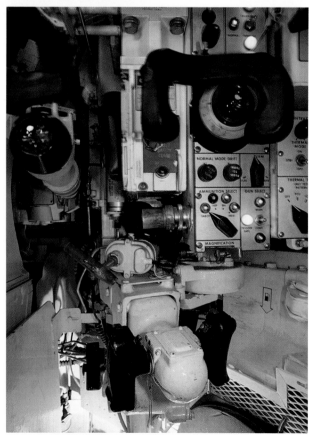

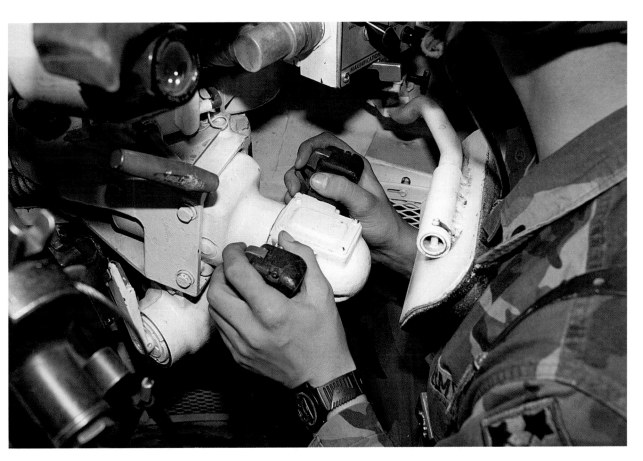

The sight systems are all powered up and adjusted, the cannon is bore-sighted, and the proper data entered into the ballistic computer. Turn the Weapon Select switch to MAIN for the cannon. Press your CVC against the pad around the sight - you can see the world outside.

Grasp the Cadillacs with both hands and depress the lower triggers on the front of each grip; these are the 'paddle switches' which power up the turret motors. Rotate the grips to the left - the turret will swing to the left, faster or slower, depending on the amount of deflection you induce. Rotate the grips slightly backwards - the sight image begins to elevate. With these simple-seeming hand controls you can point the cannon precisely.

Select Thermal Mode switch to ON, Polarity to WHITE HOT - you can now see in the dark, through smoke or fog. Set the magnification control under the eyepiece to 3X for wide field, then use your hand controls to

scan the battlefield. Let's say you spot a couple of targets: a cruising enemy T-72, followed at a discreet distance by a BMP personnel carrier. You are cleared to engage both. The tank is the greater threat, at about 2,500 meters, so engage him first.

You call 'Tank and PC, front' on the ICS. Switch to 10X magnification. Moving it in a 'G' pattern, center the graticule - a small dot and crosshair pattern in the middle of the sight picture - on the tank, and track it with your controls. At the same time, press one of the laser range finder buttons on the top inside of the Cadillacs. The range will appear, measured in meters, in the lower part of your sight, and will be automatically input to the computer.

The TC calls 'Tank and PC front - Gunner, sabot, tank - HEAT, PC - tank first!', telling you that he wants you to take out the tank first with APFSDS, then the personnel carrier with

High Explosive. You respond by calling, 'Identified'.

Track the target as it moves, keeping the graticule on the vehicle's 'center of mass'. The fire control systems use the range information and tracking speed, plus all the other factors fed into the computer, to offset the actual cannon point-of-aim; just as long as you keep the graticule on the target the correct lead and elevation will be adjusted continuously until you fire.

'Lase' the target again - the range is now down to 2,000 meters, slightly over a mile, and the computer is updated automatically. You're ready to fire. The ammunition select switch is set to SABOT. The loader calls 'Up'!; the TC calls 'Fire!'; you call 'On the way!' as you squeeze the triggers on the upper front of the hand grips.

The Abrams lurches slightly, you hear a dull thump, and the sight is momentarily obscured by smoke and dust from the muzzle blast. Then you see the bright dot of the tracer element

in the sabot streak downrange, and strike the T-72 just above the turret ring - and the whole target tank suddenly disassembles as its internal ammunition detonates.

Now call 'PC, front, HEAT!', and the loader will have a high explosive round in the breech within five seconds. Switch the ammunition type to HEAT. The loader calls 'Up!'; acquire the BMP in your sight, adjust for center-of-mass, and track. Lase the BMP for range - 1,800 meters. Note that the BMP has just launched one of the new Sagger 3 wire-guided missiles at you, an accurate and effective weapon for which you are well within range.

Call 'On the way!' as you press the triggers. The HEAT round is slower, with a higher trajectory; you see the tracer streak away again, and this target also comes unglued, engulfed in blast and fire. The Sagger, suddenly left without guidance, flops to the ground to your front.

0890

(**Above**) The thermal sight picture; the graticule is centered on an M1, and the range is displayed at the bottom. Note the relatively clearer picture when compared with that of the older style image intensification passive night sight (**opposite top**).

Bryan Whalen: 'The farthest I have successfully engaged targets is three klicks. The target is amazingly small at that range, even with 10x magnification. The graticule just about covers up a tank at that range; you have to turn down the graticule brightness to see past it at that range, to see the target at all.'

(**Left & opposite below**) The 120mm gun of an M1A1 firing in daylight. The fireball is highly visible, and apart from the dirt raised by the muzzle blast jets of dust fly out of every cranny on the outside of the vehicle.

The commander

The TC's seat is a few feet behind the gunner's in the right side of the turret, but higher up. Except when actually engaging the enemy you won't spend a lot of time in this seat; fold the back down, and it turns into a platform. Climb up on it, and your head and shoulders are exposed. The big M2 .50cal machine gun is mounted just in front of your hatch.

The hatch cover can be tilted all the way back, or it can be set horizontally but raised above your head, to provide overhead cover while still allowing you a gap through which to scan the surroundings. This new generation of commander's hatches were born of the age-old reluctance to 'button up' and rely on periscopes until the very last moment before combat - miscalculation of that moment has killed countless commanders. The fully open position affords the best visibility but the least protection against artillery airbursts. The 'open-protected' position allows good all-around visibility but restricts vision overhead. There are no perfect choices in this life. In action the TC will pop up and down from the open hatch, looking around for threats and danger areas and targets, then sliding back down to use his sights and his override controls.

(**Above**) In the slanting rays of early morning Sgt.Gordon Tom, TC, checks for hostiles in 'the Valley of Death' at the National Training Center.

(**Left**) Lt.Chris Brown, USMC 1st Tank Bn., in the more frigid surroundings of Yakima, Washington; note the CVC helmet, fire retardant gloves, and the body armor - in standard BDU-finish cover - worn over the tank coveralls.

(**Opposite**) Ultimately, no technological wizardry can make the Mark I eyeball redundant.

(Above) Together with his navigation, command and communications functions, the TC is always responsible for protecting the front and right quadrants from threats with his .50cal, which has a 360 degree field of fire; the loader's skate-mounted M240 only has an arc of 265 degrees.

(Opposite top) The M1 gunner's and, right, commander's stations seen from the loader's position, here with the TC's seat back folded down.

(Left) From the same viewpoint, the TC looking through his GPS Extension sights and holding the CPC override handgrip. Ahead of it is the remote control grip for his .50cal machine gun.

(Opposite below) The inside of TC's position, looking upwards from the gunner's seat.

Nine times out of ten, the gunner will find the target first - except in the new M1A2, with its improved optics for the commander. On the A2 the TC will find the enemy first most of the time.

When you spot a target, you continue your scan for a moment to make sure there isn't something closer - a tank might come up over a rise. Call 'Target, tank!'; the gunner will respond 'Identified!'; the TC continues his scan, then issues his fire command - 'Gunner, sabot, tank!' As soon as the gunner has the target in his sight he lases the target, aligns the graticule, and switches over to the GAS. Since the GAS has line-of-sight with the gun tube, the gunner uses it to verify that the tube has a clear shot and that there aren't any obstructions.

In a defensive engagement you'll normally be sitting in a hull-down position, with just the sights exposed. Nobody will be able to spot you like that. If the engine is running there's a chance an enemy might pick up your thermal signature, but that's unlikely with most threat tanks like the T-72.

(continued on page 52)

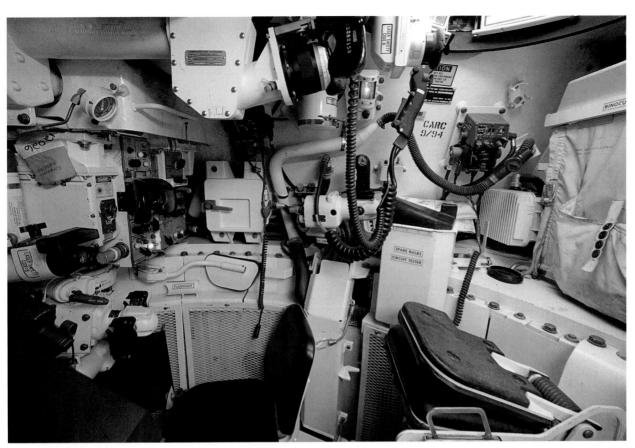

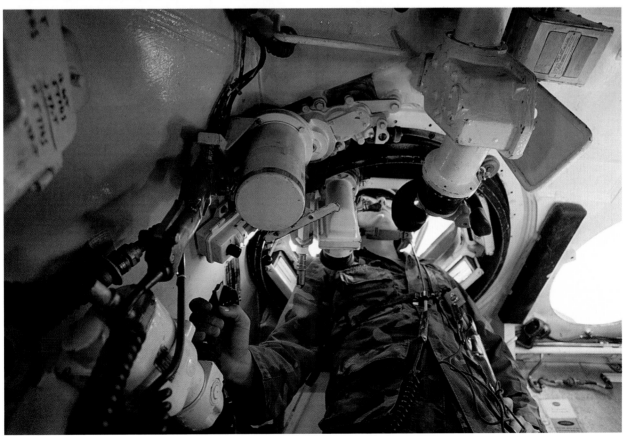

51

Next you call 'Driver, move out! Gunner, take over!' - and the driver moves the tank forward up out of its hole, raising the gun over the berm. Normally the driver will have the tank in gear, his foot on the brake, ready to execute the pop-up manoeuver; and a good driver will shift out of drive and into neutral, allowing the vehicle to glide to a stop instead of jerking it to a halt with the brakes. Even though the gun tube is stabilized the driver tries to avoid any movement that might knock the gun out of perfect alignment. Even if the gun doesn't get misaligned the gunner's head might be moved by a sudden stop, slowing down the engagement.

The moment the gun tube is clear of the berm the gunner orders 'Driver, stop!'; the gunner's hands never leave the Cadillacs, and the graticule should remain on the target. The gunner fires by depressing one or both of the two triggers on the front of his control handles. If he misses - and he sometimes will - he calls, 'Re-engage!'; if he kills the target - as almost always happens - the call is 'Target!' If there are no more targets to engage in his sector, the TC will order 'Gunner, cease fire. Driver, back up.'

Tim McDonald, a TC with the Marines' 4th Tank Battalion, explains how he worked during the Gulf War:

'My unit, First Platoon, Bravo Company, 4th Tank Battalion, participated in the attack into Kuwait City, attached to 1st Battalion, 8th Marines.

'We normally moved in wedge formation - First Platoon leading, with Second and Third to the left and right, offset behind us, with the company commander and XO in the middle. This movement technique worked great.

'Sometimes we had Cobras supporting us in these attacks from right overhead, no more than 50 feet or so. They'd dash out, take a look for us, then back off and tell us where the enemy targets were.

'We took a few hits, but only small arms fire. Actually, it was kind of tough to tell because our tanks got pretty well chewed up during the advance - I went over some cars, and through a few buildings ... The tanks were brand new when we got them, but they were pretty beat up when we were done with them.

'When I identified an enemy tank I called the other tanks in the platoon with the report "Contact, tank, front" - that told them I was getting ready to shoot a tank; then I popped back inside, and called "Gunner, sabot, tank - Fire sabot!" You need to be inside the tank when the gun fires - the wash from the blast kicks up so much dust that you can't see your hit. But with the thermal you get a momentary flash, then you can watch your round go downrange.

'We aim for "center-of-mass", right below the turret ring. T-72s stow the propellant and projectiles down at the bottom of the hull, and once you get a hit in that area, the tank is done for - the ammunition detonates and blows the turret off the tank, like a cork coming out of a bottle. The effect is instantaneous. For example, I fired on a T-72 at 1,140 meters. When I hit it, I noticed something fly off, but didn't think any more about it. A couple of days later we went over to inspect the damage; the turret had flown off and landed on its side next to the tank - that's what I had seen.'

(**Opposite**) Abrams TC - note shoulder patch of 4th Infantry Division – scanning the surroundings through his cupola periscopes while keeping hold of his override control stick. Note details of his CVC helmet, comms rig and shoulder-holster, and the butt of the M16 rifle stowed just beyond his right leg. The sight immediately below the red cupola crank handle is for his .50cal MG; that to the left of it is his GPS Extension for the main gun.

(**Right**) Remote aiming and firing of the commander's .50cal from 'under armor'.

(**Below**) The view through the optical sight for the TC's .50cal.

Drills and Tactics

An individual Abrams tank is a sophisticated, elegant, expensive, and extremely vulnerable target when left to its own devices. A pair of Abrams working as a team can complete some basic armor missions. A platoon of M1s, with a competent leader and with reasonable missions, is a fearsome force. And a full-up company of Abrams, with attached mechanized infantry and working as a 'combined arms team', is quite capable of sweeping through most obstacles to its progress to be found on modern battlefields.

The key to the successful employment of any weapon is co-ordinated, disciplined, precision use. Individual tank crews, sections and platoons practice their moves with carefully scripted scenarios called battle drills. These train all the individuals in a unit to react almost automatically in a given situation.

Movement techniques

Tank tactics are based very much on threat levels. When a commander is confident that there is no chance of meeting an enemy the formation may blast down a road or trail in formation, one behind the other, in a movement technique called 'travelling'. If contact with the enemy is possible but not very likely and speed is important, the commander will order 'travelling overwatch'; this puts a rearguard on the end of the column.

When contact with the enemy is likely 'bounding overwatch' is employed. Half the unit - e.g. one section of a platoon - will halt, scan for targets, and engage any enemy that appear. At the same time the other half will bound forward, staying well within the

(continued on page 56)

(**Above**) 'Travelling overwatch' - M1s of 2-35th Armor, 4th Infantry Div., Fort Carson.

(**Left**) Typical dawn activity at the Tactical Operations Center, National Training Center, Fort Irwin. An Abrams unit of the US Marine Corps is going to be out in the desert today, working up its movement techniques and battle drills.

(**Opposite**) The cold start of a long day for SSgt.Rick Freier, USMC 4th Tanks. Note hatch and machine gun mount details.

protective range of the overwatching section's guns, until they stop in their turn. The forward section prepares to engage any enemy while the trail element moves up to join the lead.

The separate elements can either leapfrog, alternating in the lead, or the commander may order successive bounds, particularly when he wants to maintain control of the route of movement. Then he will lead the platoon or company, moving ahead in short but well-guarded bounds, while the other element follows and provides support.

Fire commands

Because of the speed and precision required during combat with enemy armor, a tank crew drills long and hard on its fire commands and procedures. These commands will normally be issued by the TC, who has the best visibility, and have a ritual sequence: alert, weapon, description of the target, location of the target, control measures, execution.

The platoon leader spots a target and wants to engage, so he first warns part or the entire platoon to prepare to fire. He calls 'Contact!' if he wants the whole platoon to fire, or 'Alpha' or 'Bravo' if he wants only one section to engage. He might even want just a single tank to fire, calling 'One Bravo' to indicate the platoon sergeant's tank.

He then indicates the weapon or ammunition to be used - sabot, HEAT, coax - although this is optional. He will probably already know what's in the breech of each cannon, having indicated his choice for 'battlecarry'. Next he identifies the target type, e.g. 'Six tanks'; and where they are - 'TRP (terrain reference point) Three'. Then he can, if he wants, indicate who is to shoot at what: if he calls 'Cross' the tanks fire a crossing pattern, with the left-hand target being engaged by the right-hand Abrams. Finally, he can give the fire command: 'At my command - Fire!'

In practice, it sounds like this: 'Contact - Sabot - Six tanks, TRP Three - Cross - At my command - Fire!' During those few seconds the gunners in all four tanks find the target, acquire it, lase it, wait for an 'Up' from the loader; the gunners call 'On the way!' and press the triggers on the platoon leader's command.

That's what the Armor School says is supposed to happen, and that's what the crews get tested on. But the American soldier, left to his own devices, will quickly modify any such ritual, either to be more efficient or for simple amusement. For example, some crews will occasionally use Beavis & Butthead or Star Trek-style fire commands during training. But a more common modification simply pares the commands down to a bare minimum, based on a procedure called 'battlecarry'.

Battlecarry

Tank crews pre-load and index the main gun for anticipated threats. For example, if a unit expects to engage tanks the TC will announce to his crew, 'Battlecarry sabot; battle sight one-two-hundred.' The loader loads a sabot round and calls 'Sabot loaded'; the gunner selects SABOT on the ammunition type switch, manually enters 1200m as the range, then reports, 'Sabot indexed.' The TC looks through his Gunner's Primary Sight Extension, verifies that the 1200 meter range is entered, then calls to the crew, 'Battle sight one-two-hundred.' Now, when the crew first encounters the enemy, the critical first shot will go downrange several seconds faster.

(continued on page 61)

A pair of 'missile magnets' - a command group of US Marine 'tracks', variants of the big LVTP-7 Amphibious Assault Vehicle. These are excellent for getting Marines ashore, but are not designed or built to survive land encounters with serious armored opposition, and should not be considered as true APCs.

Abrams advancing in strength across part of the Mojave Desert training area around Twentynine Palms, California. The US forces are fortunate in having wide open spaces for realistic training; these are becoming scarce in crowded Europe, and British tankers do much of their live-fire training on the vast Canadian prairies.

59

Action Drills

Abrams crews also conduct 'action drills' to rehearse the way they respond to any threats that suddenly appear. The platoon commander must only give a very minimum of orders to his subordinate tanks - if he turns, everybody turns. He orders the platoon into various combat formations, depending on the tactical situation, and the other TCs and drivers react immediately.

For example, a platoon may be moving down a trail when enemy 'dismounts' are observed nearby. The platoon leader will call 'Contact, Troops, West, Fire!'; the platoon continues moving but all the turrets turn toward the threat and engage with coax and .50 calibre. If an enemy tank is spotted to the front, he may order 'Contact, Tank, North! Action Front!' - and the platoon automatically shifts to line-abreast formation while individual tank commanders and gunners engage the target.

Action drills are also used to automatically shift direction of travel or formation. Without saying a word the platoon leader can turn off a trail to his left, and the other three tanks will automatically turn left at the same time, into a line-abreast formation, and continue moving. Every tank keeps its place in the formation but the unit reacts to change in the terrain or to threats without orders or halts. The commander will generally help out with arm or flag signals if he's not buttoned up, but these are unecessary; the tanks should all slide into their spots without banging into each other - a neat trick in the middle of a dark and stormy night ...

TANKER'S GLOSSARY

Agony wagon Ambulance

Amtrac USMC Amphibious Assault Vehicle

Angry-X Any AN/GRC-X radio, e.g. AN/GRC-19.

ASS Armor School Solution

Beaucoup and Schwanzig A whole bunch ('as in the number of T-72s we were expected to stop with one M60A3').

BFG Big ******* Gun; also, BFH (hammer), BFW (wrench), BFR (rocks), etc.

Bitch plate The engine access plate on the rear deck, partially blocked by the turret overhang even when traversed, and thus a bitch to replace.

Blivet Rubber fuel bag

Brain bucket CVC helmet

Bush bunnys Infantry; also, grunts, crunchies, speed bumps, human mine detectors, and if feeling really hostile, track grease.

Bustle rack Stowage area outside rear of turret.

Cheater pipe (or bar) Chromium pipe used for leverage on T-slides and ratchets.

Cherry driver, etc. Crewman new to his job.

Cherry juice Red turret hydraulic oil.

Deadlined Unserviceable vehicle or equipment; also, unproductive individual.

Dismount Anybody on foot; usually, people in your line of sight, e.g. 'Dismounts with RPGs to your right front - watch out!'

Disneyland Disney Barracks Complex, Fort Knox, KY

Dogbone Roadwheel lifting arm

Donkey dick Spout for 5-gallon gas can

Dragon wagon M123/M15A2 tank transporter

DU Depleted Uranium

Elephant rubber Moisture barrier bag on the combustible case of 120mm ammunition.

FIDO 'It doesn't matter' - from, '**** It, Drive On'.

First Shirt Forward Support Battalion; or, First Sergeant.

FUPP Full Up Power Pack

Granny gear Lowest transmission gear, low transfer range.

Graticule Aiming reference marks visible in gunsight 'picture'.

Ground hop kit Home-brewed device for starting tanks in the motor pool.

Hatch plug Totally incompetent crewman.

Head space & timing gauge Issued to crews for checking bolt spacing and adjusting timing of .50cal MG; the term 'head space and timing' is also used when questioning somebody's capabilities.

Heat High Explosive Anti-Tank

Heavys Tanks

Highboy M577 Command Post track

Hog palace Senior NCOs' lounge (now called the Rocker II) at Fort Knox.

Hole Driver's compartment

Hull down Tank at rest in such a position that the hull is concealed, allowing target acquisition with minimum exposure.

Kinderpanzer 'Baby tanks' - M2/M3 Bradley infantry fighting vehicles.

LID Lost In Desert - something you don't want to happen while at the NTC.

Little Joe 3.5in. open end wrench for the idler arm; also referred to auxiliary power unit in pre-M60 days.

Ma Deuce M2 .50cal machine gun

Machts nicht poles 'Don't matter poles' - black and white plastic poles marking the sides of roads in Federal German Republic.

MBT Main Battle Tank

Mike Golf Usual radio callsign for company or battalion Master Gunner; when called over the radio it means someone has a problem they want him to fix.

Mover Moving target

MRS Quickie Muzzle Reference Sensor (boresight) check, carried out regularly to fine tune main sight adjustment.

Pacing the trace Border patrol in Federal Republic of Germany.

Powerwagon Truck, cargo, 3/4-ton, 4x4

Prick-X Any AN/PRC-X radio, e.g. AN/PRC-10 .

Sabot 105mm or 120mm smoothbore cannon round with discarding 'shoe'; from the French. Generic term for Kinetic Energy ammunition.

Slow movers Helicopters

Stumps Stupid Tankers Under Maintenance Protection - broken down.

Swab job Bore-cleaning brush mounted on jeep to clean bores of many tank guns quickly in a depot or other facility.

Taking a HEAT round Getting chewed-out, usually by First Sergeant or above.

Tanker roll Blanket and sleeping bag (w/mosquito net in season) rolled as tightly as possible, wrapped in shelter-half to keep dry, tied with 'spaghetti' straps, and stowed in the bustle rack.

Tanker's bar Pry bar - see Cheater.

Tinker tankers M551 Sheridan crews, from their maintenance-heavy and breakdown-prone vehicle.

Tracks Generic term for tracked AFVs other than tanks and SP artillery - infantry carriers, command post vehicles, etc.

Track pads Oval breaded veal patties served at Fort Knox mess halls. Similar in appearance but allegedly inferior in flavor to the rubber pads found two to each track link on M60 and M1 MBTs.

Travel lock Anything facing the wrong way (as in 'Get that hat out of travel lock, soldier!')

Turret counseling Squaring away an unsatisfactory tanker in an informal manner away from the protective eyes of senior ranks.

Turret down Tank at rest in such a position that its full height to the turret top is concealed in dead ground.

Turret monkeys Turret mechanics (also turret rats, wrench monkeys).

TWAT Tanker without a tank.

Unass the AO (verb) To leave an area hurriedly (i.e. 'I'm getting my ass out of this Area of Operations.')

Universal socket set A crescent wrench.